Ripples on a Stream

Poems and artwork by

Loretta Proctor

Matador
9 Priory Business Park,
Wistow Road, Kibworth Beauchamp,
Leicestershire. LE8 0RX
Tel: 0116 279 2299
Email: books@troubador.co.uk
Web: www.troubador.co.uk/matador
Twitter: @matadorbooks

ISBN 978 1788036 290

British Library Cataloguing in Publication Data.
A catalogue record for this book is available from the British Library.

Typeset in 11pt Minion Pro by Troubador Publishing Ltd, Leicester, UK

Matador is an imprint of Troubador Publishing Ltd

Life's journey has never been a straight line for me but a spiral, sometimes upwards, sometimes down. These poems and drawings began when I was fourteen and express the emotions and feelings encountered on the journey so far. As an only child whose parents moved frequently, I was thrust upon my inner resources. My father was a wonderful artist but very little remains of his work. However, his artistic genes were in me and I began to draw mandalas and esoteric drawings as a child. They gave me a sense of intense satisfaction and peace. When I studied the writings of Carl Jung later in life, I was astonished to find that these are archetypes that spring from our deepest realms. Tapping these profound, hidden areas of the psyche has always been a rich source of creativity and joy to many. I hope that I have managed to express something of the inexpressible in this little book and that it may resonate with the experiences of others.

Please do visit my website at *www.lorettaproctor.com*

contents

Ripples on a Stream

Life's but a sigh among the treetops,
A ripple on a never-ending stream.
What is it worth to have a great ambition?
Our little thoughts, ephemeral as a dream,
Soon, soon effaced from Time's poor memory,
Erased, forgotten, fleeting every word.
All that is wise and lovely now will fade away
And in another age will be no longer heard.

There have been many ages and been many men.
A thousand now are scattered in the earth.
Earth to earth, none knows where they are gone.
They have returned to that which gave them birth.
Though in each age were some who found their fame
Yet there were many who were never known.
These are the ones that dwell now in the clay.
And their names never will be shown.

We suffer but we soon forget.
Laughter's a fallen petal on the stream
That floats away beyond us
And carries all to that eternal theme.

Our buds will open and we'll spring to bloom
When that first blush of sunshine gilds our leaves.
Our petals scatter, mingle with the dust
And all in dust's achieved.

But there is always that Immortal core
That like a bird is fluttering deep within.
And when we meet the earth, it will spring forth.
To meet its origin.

Ripples on a stream

The Going Down

And now the daisies say goodnight
Fold up their arms, turn off the light,
Hide away heart, bow down their head,
Turn in their leaves and go to bed.
Skywards the swooping swifts do beat
Their wings against the summer heat
And arc their way between the space
Of narrow walls bedecked with lace,
Gossamer of spiders' webs; forgotten thread
From which the erstwhile occupants have fled.
Mellow softness in the sun's last gleam
Warms now still leaves about the stream
And streaming rays break up gold bars;
Anticipation of the coming stars,
Making a dance of diamonds, speckled glow,
That rosy-coloured gleams
    on the down flow
       of slithering, slow moving
         fishes in the deep;
           while slowly, slowly, Nature's world
            sinks
              fast asleep.

Life

Well, what is Life, is it just a dream?
For some I think it's so.
They think they're alive but their souls are dead
And it's time they got to know.

You're only free when your heart at last,
Shakes off the binding chains of its past.
When you learn to forget and you learn to forgive,
It's only then you begin to live.
You're only free when your soul is free,
Not wrapped in mental poverty.
When your heart's an ocean full of love
And Time's eternity.

You learn to live when you learn to give.
It's only then you're free.

Oh to be free!

Oh to be as free as air
On a great sea-shore.
Dance upon the waves and share
Their fragrance evermore.
Drift above the changing tides
Like a seagull in the sky,
Live amongst the coral caves,
Never, never die.
Free, oh ever free!
That's how I wish to be.

Flying Free

Bird Thoughts

There's such a twittering of birds about the lilac buds,
Like little thoughts chasing each other
In and out the branches of the mind;
Restless, febrile movements.
They're after the bread I put out on the lawn.
And the great starlings –
Greedy birds! They chase away the tiny sparrows
From their due share of bounty;
Just as large woes will chase away one's little hopes,
Devouring one's substance
As hungrily as starlings fighting over bread.

Contemplating Future Identities

Leaving the echoing eddies of my life behind me,
Behind me on Life's ever ebbing shore,
Becoming once again a bud, a chrysalis,
Full of new potentials held in store,
I'll sleep awhile as sleep the just, the innocent,
Returning when Creation wills me into life once more.
But will it all be new and wondrous as my heart hopes?
Or am I destined to be once again….

A Painted Lady, Peacock butterfly?

May I not next time round be Admiral or Emperor?
Maybe a Skipper or a Queen of Spain?
Even to be a Gatekeeper would make a happy change.
(To be like Janus and gaze either way would be most strange!)
Well, at least, let's try another role or two.
A Camberwell Beauty or a Duke of Burgundy,
A Tiger Hawk perhaps?
Or even just a simple ordinary moth would do!

Capturing Reality

The shifting phantasmagoria of experience
Greets this eye that gazes through this window;
A window looking out on Life.

Part of this strange abode I call my house;
This house has windows open day and night,
It doesn't want to sleep.

How long have any of us left to sleep away our life
And waste the brightness of the Day,
The sweetness of the Night?

The memory awakens that I loved You once
And knew You too. It seems so far away.
A lifetime long ago.

I'm running wild and searching here and there.
Around each corner shifts another face or form;
Melting, dissolving, insubstantial.

Where will I find You in this dream,
Which these strange floating ghosts about my heart

Call Life?
Yet, fleetingly I catch a moment's glimpse.
If I could only hold it as one freezes forms
On photographic plates.

Could say 'I have it. Now I know the answer to this life?'
And really look at it and see what's there.
But it eludes me still

And maybe always will.

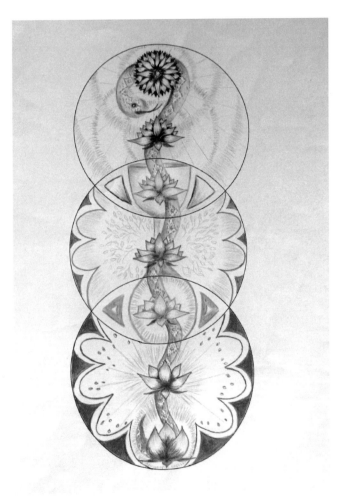

Kundalini Serpent

Eternal Shapes

Sweet Robin Redbreast!
Pictures on postcards of illusory festivity
These are not you, amidst imaginary snow.
Rather, I'll meet you in my rainy garb
While digging the potato patch.

Though you may make me feel the wrapping round
Of winter chills,
Yet bright and cheerful is your form,
Your rosy waistcoat and your lucid eyes,
Gazing on me, head cocked from side to side,
Considering if I'm safe to know
And if the slicing spade has turned
Up worms enough to make good supper time.
You make me smile with joy
And that is rare enough these days.

I feel such love for little birds.
Their tiny, tender forms
So light, so floaty-delicate and weak,
They could be crushed by one ferocious blow.

Yet, strong enough to lift up on the wildest winds
And go their chosen way;
They're never blown about like leaves
Are blown hither, thither.

Looking on every bird I marvel,
For they are ageless, timeless, never changing beings.
Still the same redbreast hops beside my spade
As the one yesteryear I knew when I was young.
Perhaps the very bird that Adam pointed gleefully to Eve.
Only the forms pass on, I know not where –
For where do dead birds go? You seldom see them.
All I know, my pretty Robin, is that
You're the self-same bird
That's been there since the dawn of time.

The Waiter

Impatient, weary and care-laden man,
Who tramps the platform in an anguished way,
Urging within the slow, reluctant train,
Why not sit still and watch the sparrows play?
The whole of Nature chirps and hops with glee
Among the sleepers and the carefree weeds,
Yet Man just yearns to get from A to B
And wants to fly there at the swiftest speeds,
His thoughts already lost in papers grey,
His dreary files and faces blank and wan,
Surrounded by the whirr and click that rules his day,
The great machines that take the place of men.
And, having got there, what does he do then?
He yearns impatient to be home again.

Old Books Upon My Bookshelf

Rubies and emeralds they are
Resting among the brown and upright leather pillars,
Gold-dusted by the sun.
Motes in the sunbeams, playing, dancing
On dusty, gold-tooled leather spines amongst which gleam
Those of deep ruby, those dark green like emeralds,
Well used and worn, now scarcely read these ancient tomes.
Yet they're old friends upon my shelf
I wouldn't be without.

Old Books on my Bookshelf

Early Morning

It was in the early morning, blackbird song and
long wet grass, shuffling through making trails in dew
in the early mornings of my life.
Something of magic in the sun slanting
through wet, dripping branches,
pearls of water drops in spidery webs enchaining
blade to blade in the long wet grass.

It was in the early morning rising from warm sheets
when hearing that cuckoo summons from
far distant woods, calling , welcoming me forth
into the dewy day, doors unbolted, stepping from within
dark walls, shadowed kitchens, cold and stony floor.
Stepping forth and catching at my heart.
They were.
Sun's rays, dewy grass, pearls of water drops.

The Real Me, where's she?

The tangled web we weave
that we call Life
in which we practise busily to deceive
and fill with strife,
Right from the start,
right from the start, we know
the Truth that's in our heart's
not always what we show.
But we invent our structures every day
and they don't take us far.
Instead they lead us miles away
from who we really are.

The Skier

Standing on top a silent mountain range
Snow rivers flowing, quivering and shining white
Before my dazzled eyes and tumbling down the slopes
That spread before me.
Eager the white snow waits
As if with breath held in for my impetuous flight.
And yet I linger. I cannot move because absorbed
By sunbeams' glittering light along the valley floor.

I hover still, poised on the edge of Time;
A pause that stretches an eternity of awe.
Then of a sudden, in one swift, wide and uplifting arc
I fling myself away into the void below
And downhill crunch and whistle on my skis.
With plunging sticks and flying hair, I carve my way
Through rivulets of snow.
And at the bottom of the slope on looking back
I see the dark, cruel furrow that the scything path has cut
Into that pristine, sparkling carpet, white and pure.

And see the mountain rise without complaint up to the
skies
And dwarf my feeble self with sheer immensity of size.

Forgotten

Rain beating on the ground.
Swift eddies flowing into gutters,
Sticks swirling in the mud flow,
Umbrellas popping up like mushrooms.

I saw the girl slumped on the ground;
A shivering body soaked by creeping rain.
Behind her bending back, shop windows lure
Us in with lights hurt-bright
And goods that glitter, tempting passers-by.
We stop and look, a mindless fleeting moment
Then following the crowd, move on.

Oh, that relentless stream of people!
A stream that casts humanity aside
Like flotsam on a wintry bank
In pouring rain.

I never did go back to her
That girl sat silent in the rain.
I wanted to but then forgot.

Growing Up

Little sad child, you peep out from adult eyes,
Needy from his blue ones, enraged from her brown,
Bewildered from my looking glass.
Deep need and fearful anguish are your lot.
Are you to be abandoned on a doorstep somewhere
By mothers who cannot contain your infant rage?
Mothers yourselves, you feed your babes with milk-hate;
Fathers yourselves, you give your sons a sword.
Where does it end, this sadness, where transmute?
Where does it go this cry of pain and need?

Somewhere in the depths of our own being
There lies a coal-black jewel.
Leave it; it becomes a diamond in the end.
But better still, turn it to white hot flame,
That burning dross can purify these hardened hearts.

Rising isn't easy, sinking down is all we know.
Even getting out of bed's not easy; we want to sleep forever.

But wake and rise we must.
Soar upwards, take that dark jewel with us.
Let it ignite the dormant sleeper in our heart
And free the Love within.

Captive Fire

I capture a butterfly in a net for a while,
Admiring its fiery loveliness, its colour.
Its wings are vast for such a slender form.
I cannot keep it; how keep so beautiful a thing?
It's realms are in the air and in the sun
Darting restlessly, seeking and searching
From flower to flower.

To keep it, I would need to pin it down
And then be left with something dead.

I need perhaps to grow my wings and fly away with it,
Stop crawling so contented on the earthy realm
But take the flight away with it, towards the Sun,
Towards the Self. Ah butterfly!
Your life is brief but glorious!

Solar Fire

I Had a Dream

'I had a dream,' the great man said.
He had a dream of love and faith
A time would come for men to live
In harmony,
He said.
He had a dream.

I had a dream too, long ago,
A dream of love and beauty.
A longing to be where
The green things grow
Abundantly.
I had a dream.

My dream came true, the dream I had.
I look out on the hills and vales.
I look out on a garden.
Gazing on Eden,
That's what I see
Out there.

A glorious garden full of plants,
A garden full of trees and flowers,
A garden where my soul delights
To spend its hours.
It all came true,
My dream.

If only all the world could be
A garden green with growing bliss
Where Man can live in harmony
No wars and hate and pain
But love.
A dream.

But dreams come true
Sometimes.

My Back Yard

In my back yard are growing things
and tubs of this and that.
I lean out of the window
and watch the sun go down
on my back yard.
The bats come flying from the pines.
In circles, round and round,
they skirt the trees
and make their squeaky sound,
the bats in my back yard.
Just listen to that last, sweet chirp
of blackbirds fluting song,
as sleepy birds now roost.
I listen for a long, long time
and watch the sun go down,
peaceful and tranquil
in my back yard.

No, Dylan Thomas!

No, Dylan Thomas – you are very wrong.
It is not on this earth that we belong.
You should go gentle into that good night
You should not rage against the dying of the light,
Nor cling to all the pain and misery of being mortal.
But step in peace and glory through that joyous portal.

Four Elements Mandala

Imagination

If I could only once escape
And burst the shackles of this world
And like a bird to fly and fly
beyond the horizon into the sky!
Imagination's a new world
And into it I will retreat
And there will be no boundaries.
I'll go where I will, do as I please.

Circular Feelings

I can see him sitting there
gazing and gazing at me.
He loves me so, he doesn't care
that all the world can see.
Yet I know that when he asks me
if I love him too,
I must answer sadly
that this I cannot do.
I don't love him though I try
and when I see his face
falling, it will make me cry
feeling in his place.
For I love somebody too
who doesn't care for me.
If I ask him how *he* feels
he'll smile in sympathy,
For he's in love with someone else,
someone who doesn't care.
Isn't it a sorry world, with nobody to pair?

Solar Eclipse

He who was like the sun to me
Has gone.
The fair, the smiling face that shone for me
Now gone.
An eclipse has happened suddenly,
I sit in the dark and cannot see.
A lost child.
All gone.

Please put on the light someone
And come and comfort me.
It's wrong to leave a child alone
Sobbing so bitterly.
What hope has such a little one,
Without a tender friend?
Come, share my pain an hour or two
And help this heart to mend.
Be at my side and hold me near
For lost love leaves its mark.
We are all God's little ones
Sobbing in the dark.

Is this the End?

It's dead, it's gone;
And like a cock that crows at midnight
Out of tune with nature and itself,
So you and I no longer are in tune.
No longer yearn to meet, to love
To care.

There is no caring
Anymore.
And so it goes.
It's Life
It's Love.
It's over.

On Gullets Quarry in a Rainstorm

High on the hills the clouds come storming
Darkened by raindrops falling thick as hail
Upon the flooding stones; rivulets
Like streams of life blood forming
The clear waters of the springs
Rushing their headlong way into the vale.

Here on these mystic hills the waters gush
Pure and immaculate, riding rock and stone,
Cascading downwards to unfathomable gullies
To fill strange, silent pools where winds do hush
Amongst the blasted quarries left by men,
Where foolish bathers with their lives atone.

Those poor, dead souls, a sacrifice made to the gods
Of strange insensibility. Then hills as soft and
Smoothly rounded as a woman's breast were scarred
And gouged out by the work of men to lay the roads
Of endless human traffic through the land.
They now remain deep, icy pools of death.

Still Dancing

In wild, wild moments there's the rush of wind
Upon my face, streaming out strands of hair
As I run down hills of mind on lissom legs,
Twigs snapping under my feet while I remain
Childlike and playful, blissful and unaware.
But all this in my mind because
I cannot do this barefoot running anymore.
Can't run at all. Those days of mad abandon gone.
But I can still walk slowly on the nice neat paths
Among the bluebells and my heart can still
Skip, dance and jump for joy and sing its song.

Beginnings

Sweet Sorrow

Sometimes briefly, sometimes deep, I tap
into those slow-moving thrilling rhythms
but only when I am with you.
You open my heart, my eyes with a mere touch
of fingers,
A mere touch; fragile moments of delight
soon enough gone as summer goes with the first
lingering cloud, or tumbling shower of rain.
Your moods, your eyes enfold me, wrap me round
as leaves enfold the calyx of an opening flower.
Nothing I can say can even half express
the deep and aching mystery of Love,
That stream of sweetness flowing to my heart;
Unsatisfied longing, it makes me ache inside,
so sweet, it makes me ache inside
the moment that we part.

The Gorgon's Face

It's all very well having pity for those who are hurt.
But do they have pity for us?
Oh, no, they fling their poison
From an overflowing cup of hate
Reducing us to nothing
Like themselves.
It hurts to meet the Gorgon, full on,
See her face.
That awesome, awful face; Kali herself looks out on me.
I've met her now;
No longer full of fear
But, oddly, tenderness
And empathy and sorrow too
For her deep pain, humiliation, grief.
Her ugliness contains the oddest beauty
My beauty all her ugliness.

Young Lover

This heart's a tender vessel ready to receive this love
He pours into me.
Flow of ardour, feeling, warmth and joy!
He pours them out and with his dreams he holds me,
Nourishing the aching void, filled to the brim
To overflowing.
His love so pure, so warm, so deep and tender true.

Youthful love, gentle and lovely soul,
Your ardour and your fire warms me through.
You say you will await me,
Cross the earth to claim me?
Ah, Gabriel Oakes, will you in truth await
Your butterfly Bathsheba to the end?

Matthew Green

It had been a tiring day that day. She sat down,
staring with eyes that gazed unseeingly
at people, vacant stares everywhere
from swaying people in long, stuffy
carriages, that rocked and shook around each corner,
snaking sinuously along the dark,
defenceless passages of Under London.

But then she noticed sitting opposite her
the tall man with the studious face,
the grey eyes thoughtful and a bearded chin;
the sort of face she liked the look of.
He'd just been where she'd been, she saw the bag
in his hand with goodies from the Library.
The books he'd bought.
He'd been where she had been.

'Train is delayed' announced the disembodied
voice from nowhere and their eyes met
in humorous exchange, defences slipping,
conventions for a moment put aside in
shared dismay.

Like old friends, they began to talk,
as if it had been yesterday they met
and many yesterdays before.
As if it had been yesterday that they had been together.

The train jolted to life and rumbled on
and still they talked of books, and libraries and reading
research, writing, all the joys of life,
into the next station where startled, suddenly
aware, he rose and left the train.
'My name is Matthew Green.' he said just as he left.
She almost stretched her arms out after him.
Like Eurydice longing for her Orpheus she slipped
back into the underworld.
Just thus the stranger disappeared from her life
whose name was Matthew Green.

The City Streets at Night

Walking along the city streets at night
when all the goodly souls are well abed.
Deep, deep the quiet. Hearing footfalls, slight
ring of heels upon the hardened ground
to make me start a little at the sound,
afraid perhaps of my own shadow,
my breathing fast and hurried, full of fright.

In that still peace, that eerie silence of the night
the tall trees bend, leaves rustle in the light
and tender wind and sway to its caresses.
And in the darkened houses, weary people sleep
while eager lovers, behind half-drawn blinds, do keep,
their tryst and moan and rock and sigh,
as I do haste through city streets at night.
Then suddenly a glorious, liquid, fluid, flowing,
the warbling, trilling, swirl of notes from golden throat
of the night bird on his branch pours forth
As he sits swaying in the loving wind, his joy proclaiming.
I stop quite still and listen, captured and enthralled.
by this extraordinary sound. A bird
That sings so sweetly in the night
In city streets at night.

I was born in Eternity

I was born in Eternity
Where Mother and Father are One.
Born in the sound-filled silences of space
Where stars are made from swirling dust
And life in sudden proton meetings
Springs into being; male and female,
Atoms that split smaller, smaller ever smaller
To the never-ending core of Being.
From these I too became a Man,
Leaving my vast and luminous mansions for your sake,
Letting myself grow smaller, smaller to fit your minds;
A sperm in an egg, my beginning the same as yours.

Sons of Man, Sons of God,
I will show you how atoms come together,
Larger, larger, ever larger.
Plants, animals, men, suns, galaxies beyond time,
Growing in size and structure.
And you will grow with me through the dark tunnels of
the mind,
Slipping from Death to Life, from Dark to Light,
Till we together shall inherit
Those boundless, beautiful places
Where Father and Mother are One.

Starburst

Mary Webb's a poet but I don't think I will be

Mary Webb's a poet but I don't think I will be,
For every hour and every wind
Of ticking time does claim my mind
And dulls it down like a repetitious dropper
That wears away my silver, leaving only copper.
Busy with nothingness, with each day's need
With food to cook and babes to feed
And socks to mend and plates to clean
And oven doors that have to gleam –
For whom?…for no-one…for who cares
If dust still lingers on the stairs
Or if the ironing isn't done
Or the clock isn't wound and stops at one?
They care in the moment but that's soon past
And I've done nothing that could last.
She gave her man a torment from love's pain,
A love that crushed in yearning to be in love again.
She left her pots, she left her crocks,
She left her husband's undarned socks.
Yet would he not say all his life

How glad I am she was my wife?
How can you tend to pot and pans
And children's chatter and scratched little hands?
These everyday and much loved things
Are death, death, death to the soul that sings.
When you have to wind the clock and keep an eye on time
There simply isn't space in life to make your poem rhyme.

Written in 1983. Mary Webb wrote *Precious Bane* one of my favourite stories.

Daffodils

From the dark depths
They push up and up,
From the earth's dark bowels like a swimmer
Returning from the sea bed
With his prize of coral and pearls,
With his yearning to reach the top,
They swim up to the light.
The dark presses down upon them but cannot hold them.
They push until they burst quite suddenly into the light.
Then there's no holding them back!
Yet they're still rooted in that dark soil
As much as they may grown in the bright sun.
Their roots are in the earth and it holds them firm,
But their flowers. . . they are in the sun.
Then, when their time is over,
It's down again into the dark, dark depths,
It's down, down again into the deep, deep sleep.

Having reached Sixty Years

Well, here's an ode to this most fruitful season;
A time when I, a woman as I deem myself,
Should once, in ages past, be withered quite,
Be wrapt in black, negating all I am.
No body to be seen, a black cocoon,
Marked 'Aged Wrinkled Crone'.

In ages past I would have been.
I long for ages past when women met their fate in peace
When, from a maiden to a matron, thence to crone
Was natural transition, costumed, understood.
One played one's part and acted every role.
Now, none of us want to grow up.

Mothers, maidens, still confused, unsure,
So terrified of age and never letting go
To little wrinkles, crow's feet, laughter lines
And all the tracings of one's life upon one's face.
They strangely haven't a grey hair to show
But cream away each mark of adulthood.

My flaws, my virtues, every tiny mark
Is self-created, made from life's own stuff.
A tale to tell, a promise and a lie.
I could keep you amused and make you weep
If all the strange adventures of my heart I'd tell.
But look on me instead; it's written there.

Wisdom

Ebb and Flow

Along the vast sea shore
Eternal children play eternal games;
Lithe, moving silhouettes against the sky,
Upon the sand they write their changing names.

Lonely, detached, I wander on the sand,
Watching the waves come running to my feet
Like little children begging for a game.
Last evening's paper skeltering down the strand
Now lies beside me, just a sodden, crumpled sheet.
All news, in wet forgotten fragments, ends the same.

My feet sink down in soft and swirling sands
That curl about them, rising, beaten by the foam.
The sun makes silver points like diamonds in the waves
Like necklaces of diamonds in my hands.
So many people drifting by, so far from home;
I hear the echoing sound of children in the caves.

Shouts floating in the distance as boys play a football
game
And children dig away like little dogs or moles
As if to reach Australia; they scratch with tiny paws
But never reach their goal. It's always just the same,
For soon, so tired of trying, they leave all the great holes
For the rippling, restless sea to swallow in its maws.

Filled full of water, castles crumble into heaps,
Shell walls, banner falls, all are swept away
Later to be tossed back upon the empty beach
From which the ebbing life so quickly seeps
To be reclaimed by children of some other day
And then swept off again beyond their reach.

Along the vast sea shore
Eternal children play eternal games;
Lithe moving silhouettes against the sky,
Upon the sand they write their changing names.

Helplessness

Mother Kali came to me today
In the shape of a waif-like girl.
She held a mirror up to me
And made me see my soul.
She flung her anger over me
Just like a great, dark cloak;
And I became invisible, and I became a rock.

The grieving, frightened child I saw
Before me in this girl
Was my own infant sorrowing
And longing to be helped.
Yet I could give her nothing, not even smile at her
And when I tried to offer love,
I offered it too late.
She coldly spurned those empty words
Knowing they came from hate.

How can an empty vessel give forth water meant to heal?
How can a bath of poison cleanse a wound that has congealed?
How can a pain in one soul, comfort another's pain?
And yet, somewhere it does heal although it hurts and digs.
Like a surgeon's knife, it cuts out all the mess that we have lived.

Being and no more

Forget all the stories you've ever heard or read;
Even the ones about the saints, wise men, great souls.
They're all blind alleys, twisted paths, that lead astray,
Taking you from the reservoir, the vast depths of Now.
I watch the squirrel leaping blithely in the tree.
He only knows he is.
And so should we.

Innana's Journey

When you've been in that place where few may go
You can never be the same again.
You know yourself upside down,
You know yourself inside out.
You know yourself.

Why are people afraid?
It's a terrifying trip down there.
Of that you can be sure
As you can be of little else.
It's a dark place with howling,
Grief and pain and weeping.
Old ghosts come swirling up
To greet you, take you back.

It's a dark place down there.
You need a guide
To hold your hand and comfort you.
Ah, those dead faces, sere and gray!
They scare me.

I greet them too, I claim them,
I make my peace with them.
The dead need to be decently laid to rest.

Nothing but Talk

Sing, sing, sing, celestial choirs
And sweep this saddened soul into the stars
Which make its substance and its shape.
That I may look upon this noisy earth
Whirling about the sun yet quite forgetting
Its place amongst the spheres.

We find the soul today dry, tired and bleak.
All people can do now is write and speak.
They move hands idly over keyboards, mobile phones
All present and correct; they're there all right
And yet you find yourself
Alone and weak.
The sentimental chattering of arid minds,
For no one listens anymore and nothing binds.
They spill their puerile pathos, speak of heart and soul
But no one has a clue what these words mean.
And so they fall into the ditch together
The blind leading the blind.

Sounds flow about me and I'm under water;
Drowning in mellow, sweet voices, splendid utterances,
ideas,

Trail blazing thoughts and so called human knowledge,
But little, little of the meaning heals the heart.
I feel I live in some strange world apart
From all these learned people talking everywhere.
Their words, they fall like leaves, so dry and sere
Words that I read, words that I write, words that I hear.
I'd sooner look at lovely pictures, they're the soul –
So why not more? There should be art,
Art everywhere, pictures to open up the heart.
The heart is where the soul has fled.
We need to find it there not in the head.

Street Angel

He left me on one April day
He left me alone and in pain.
I paced the streets from nine to twelve,
Cooled by the gentle rain.
I saw his face in every man
Who passed me on the way.
I almost ran to greet them
And call them by his name.

I walked and walked until I came
To the deep riverside.
I stood upon the bridge and stared
Into the waters wide.
I saw another world below,
A world so free of care,
My desperation made me yearn
To hurl myself down there.

And then a stranger touched my arm
And gently said to me,
'Don't go there, lady, nothing in
This crazy world is free.
We have to pay a price for love
But dying doesn't do it.
Turn back and love again, my dear,
I'll help to pull you through it.'

I turned towards the silent street
I looked and looked in vain,
Who was it touched my arm that night
And walked out in the rain?
I turned away from my bleak thoughts,
Ran home across the park.
And all my life I will recall
The stranger in the dark.

First Time

Many I have loved but somehow you were first.
I think it was your hands encircling my face
Made that night special.
Funny how touch of hand on face can be so good!
Maybe because you called me by my name,
Softly, endearingly
And naming makes one feel alive and real.
Or was the secret my wet hair, fresh from the cleansing shower,
Or newness of an urgent, splendid body
Pressing on mine with joyful lustiness?
Or just the fact that you, you, you,
The One so warm, alive, compelling, broke the spell
Of crippling, ice-bound coldness in my womb?
(And afterwards you told me how I too
With undemanding giving from my heart
Freed you)

Piscean Waterways

Flowing down the riverway, I touch first one bank then
the other
For nothing stays my course. I carve my way
Through hillside, valley, slowly, gently moving.
Whatever shape I make in this I stay contained
But ever moving . . .
Moving on, restless sometimes, tumbling, cascading
In little waterfalls along the way.

Then, still and deep, I'll settle in some cosy hollow,
Rest peacefully, let other creatures rest in the soft stillness.
Everywhere I appear different, everywhere
I change my shape and sound and form
But never change the watery substance of my being.

All the rest is movement, flow and force.
My nature and my substance stays the same
And so my goal.

Nothing stops my flow towards the sea
Towards the great, encompassing Mother of my being.

Pisces Dreaming